Discover Buffalo, NY's Canalside in One Afternoon

DATES IN THE STATES

A COUPLE TRAVELING THE UNITED STATES ON A BUDGET

Mystery Date
Let's Go Buffalo!

By Dates in the States

"Our passion is travel, and we want to share our adventures to inspire others to explore the world with their loved ones. Dare to live beyond the box."

Dates in the States

Introduction

Hey there! We're Crystal and Shane, the duo behind Dates in the States, where we share our love for discovering unique adventures, unforgettable moments, and hidden gems across the U.S. Whether you're searching for a fun date idea, a new place to explore, or just a little inspiration, we've got you covered!

Our Mystery Date Books are designed to help couples (and adventurous friends!) shake up their routine and experience the best local spots in a fun, intentional way. Inside, you'll find a curated collection of date ideas. Each one meant to be completed over the course of a single day in a specific neighborhood. All of which are a surprise until you flip the page!

It's like a little challenge to break out of your comfort zone, support local, and make memories that stick. We hope this book helps you laugh more, explore more, and connect more, with each other and with your city. Let the mystery begin!

Here's What To Expect:

In this Mystery Date Book, we're taking you to Buffalo's vibrant Canalside. A lively waterfront district bursting with history, fun activities, and unforgettable dining experiences.

Here's what to expect for your day ahead:

Start your afternoon with a scenic lunch where you can enjoy waterfront views and fresh, flavorful dishes. Next, explore Buffalo's rich military history, touring historic ships and a submarine. Take a leisurely stroll along the Buffalo Canal and take a ride on a historic carousel. Take a tour to see the city from a whole new perspective before you end your day with Buffalo's famous wings.

Soak in the charm, history, and waterfront energy of Canalside. Let's dive in!

Where To Park

Shark Girl

1 Commercial St.
Buffalo, NY 14202

Skip the pricey lots when you can! During peak summer weekends or special events, parking garages can jump to $15–$25. Instead, head for Commercial Street near the Shark Girl statue. There's usually metered parking (pay at the kiosks) and sometimes it's free depending on the day. From there, it's just a short walk to get to your first few date destinations on the canal.

Don't forget to get your selfie with the Shark Girl statue! Shark Girl first appeared in 2013 and quickly became a local icon and selfie magnet. In short: she's Buffalo's unofficial waterfront mascot for offbeat charm.

1st Stop

Liberty Hound
1 Naval Park Cove
Buffalo, NY 14202

Start your Canalside date the perfect way, with lunch at Liberty Hound. This waterfront gem sits right inside the Buffalo Naval & Military Park, giving you gorgeous harbor views while you dine. On our visit, we couldn't resist their crab sandwich special, fresh, flavorful, and piled high and the chicken tacos, which were packed with bold, zesty flavor. Whether you grab a seat on the patio to soak up the breeze or settle inside for a cozy view through the windows, Liberty Hound isn't just about great food; it's about kicking off your day with Buffalo's waterfront energy all around you.

Second Stop

Naval Museum
1 Naval, Marina Park S
Buffalo, NY 14202

After lunch, take a short stroll to the Buffalo Naval & Military Park, where history comes alive right on the water. Here, you can climb aboard a collection of historic vessels, including the destroyer USS The Sullivans, the guided missile cruiser USS Little Rock, and the submarine USS Croaker. Walking through these ships feels like stepping back in time, you'll weave through narrow passageways, peek into officers' quarters, and imagine life at sea. It's a hands-on, immersive way to connect with Buffalo's military history while enjoying the incredible waterfront views.

Third Stop
Stroll the Canal

Next, take a leisurely walk along the Buffalo Canal. This scenic stretch is the perfect place to slow down and soak in the waterfront atmosphere.

From here, you'll get a different perspective on the Naval & Military Park's ships, seeing their massive silhouettes reflected in the water. Along the way, you'll find a mix of statues, memorials, and informational placards that tell pieces of Buffalo's rich history.

Whether you pause to read, snap photos, or simply enjoy the views, the canal offers a peaceful, picturesque break in your date.

Fourth Stop
Buffalo Heritage Carousel
1 Marine Dr.
Buffalo, NY 14202

Your next stop brings a touch of nostalgia. Step onto the Buffalo Heritage Carousel, a hand-carved wooden carousel originally built in 1924. After decades of delighting riders in Massachusetts, it was lovingly restored and brought to Buffalo, where it now runs entirely on solar power.

Each of its 34 animals was carefully refurbished, blending vintage artistry with modern sustainability. As you ride, you'll not only enjoy sweeping views of the waterfront, but also be part of a story nearly a century in the making.

Fifth Stop

Take a Boat Tour or Rent a Paddle

44 Prime St.
Buffalo, NY 14202

If the weather's nice and you're not ready to leave Canalside, why not take your adventure to the water?

There are plenty of ways to explore the canal: rent a canoe or kayak with BFLO Harbor Kayak, hop on a Buffalo River History Tour for a narrated journey past historic landmarks, or enjoy a more festive vibe with Big Kahuna Tiki Tours.

Whether you're paddling at your own pace or cruising along with a guide, this is the perfect way to see Buffalo from a fresh perspective before heading toward the evening.

Final Stop

Gabriel's Gate

145 Allen St.

Buffalo, NY 14201

After a full afternoon of exploring Canalside, there's no better way to cap off your date than at Gabriel's Gate.

Known for their infamous Buffalo wings, this cozy pub serves up wings that are perfectly crispy, juicy, and loaded with just the right amount of heat. Pair them with a cold drink and soak in the warm, inviting atmosphere. Whether you're sharing a plate or going head-to-head on spice level, Gabriel's Gate is a delicious finale that's quintessentially Buffalo.

Add Your Photos

Thank you for joining us on this mystery date adventure! We hope you've enjoyed the delightful experiences and memorable moments we've crafted just for you in Buffalo's Canalside.

But the adventure doesn't stop here! Keep exploring exciting mystery dates in other cities and uncover new experiences across the U.S. by visiting our website, DatesintheStates.com. There, you can purchase both physical copies and digital downloads of our mystery date books.

Plus, don't miss out on our Mystery Date Book Club, where you can receive a brand-new mystery date book every month!
Tag us in your date photos on social media! @datesinthestates

About the Creators

Crystal, the writer and creator, is a storyteller at heart. When she's not uncovering hidden gems for the next date night idea, she runs her own digital marketing company, helping small businesses improve their content marketing, increase visibility in their communities, and streamline their online presence.
Visit: crystalstatskey.com

Shane, her husband and partner in adventure, is a dedicated personal trainer and the owner of Beekstar Fitness in Irondequoit, NY. He specializes in working with clients who have limited mobility, helping them build muscle and focus on pain areas so they can regain strength and confidence in their daily lives.
Visit: beekstarfitness.com

Crystal and Shane have explored every U.S. state except Alaska (coming soon!) and are now visiting countries in alphabetical order. Whether road-tripping or curating Mystery Date experiences, they're always chasing their next adventure.

Local Love

A few local gems in Buffalo worth exploring on your next date.

THEODORE ROOSEVELT INAUGURAL NATIONAL HISTORIC SITE

FOR ALL YOU HISTORY BUFFS!

641 DELAWARE AVE, BUFFALO, NY 14202

OLDEST TREE IN BUFFALO

WE LOVE A GOOD ROADSIDE ATTRACTION

402 FRANKLIN ST, BUFFALO, NY 14202

ANCHOR BAR

BUFFALO WINGS + LIVE JAZZ

1047 MAIN ST, BUFFALO, NY 14209

Want to see your business here? See the next page for details on how to join!

Want to be featured?

MYSTERY DATE BOOK PACKAGES

—

Are you a small business looking to reach new customers? Feature your business in our next Mystery Date Book! Choose from our partnership packages below to connect with couples seeking unique experiences and exclusive deals.

Package One

LOCAL LOVE LISTING

—

A quick shoutout to show you're part of the neighborhood vibe.

Listed in the "Local Love" section of your designated neighborhood date book

Includes business name, address, and social link

Optional: Offer a small promo (e.g., 10% off for book holders)

1 social media shout-out when the book launches

$45

Package Two

FEATURE STOP

—

You're not just a business— you're part of the experience.

Marked as a "Must-Stop" on a Mystery Date

Full-page feature in the book with your story, offerings and photo

Includes 1 social media feature — a dedicated post and story highlighting your business

Note: To ensure each feature is genuine and experience-based, we require a hosted visit prior to inclusion.

$95

Package Three

PARTNER & SELLER

—

Be the spot and the source.

Everything in Tier 2

PLUS: Option to sell the Mystery Date Books at your location

Includes a bulk purchase of 10 books (yours to price + sell)

Keep 100% of the profits from in-store sales

Bonus: Have a featured "sponsored by" page and listed as an official pickup location in our promotions

$250

Prices are subject to change

Feel free to reach us at any time by sending us an email to say hi and to learn more! We look forward to hearing from you.

| www.datesinthestates.com | datesinthestatesblog@gmail.com |

Sponsors & Affiliates

Our sponsors and affiliates help make our adventures possible! Explore the amazing brands and businesses that support our community.

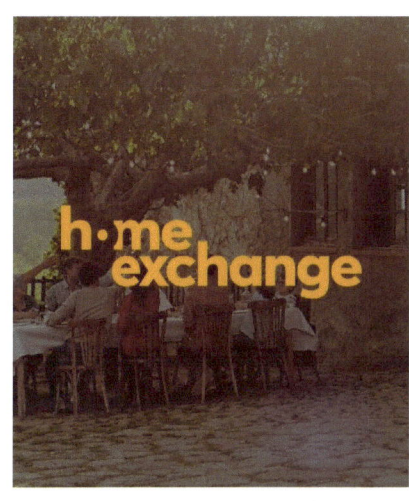

Wanderful

Wanderful is a global community for women who love to travel. Connect, explore, and join a local hub near you!

Join our Book Club!

Join our Mystery Date Book Club and be part of a travel-inspired community, discovering unique local adventures together!

HomeExchange

HomeExchange lets you swap homes with travelers worldwide for authentic, affordable stays. Join today and travel differently!

Shop our books at a store near you!

Little Button Craft
658 South Ave.
Rochester, NY 14620

The Pawsitive Cat Cafe
120 East Ave. Ste 100
Rochester, NY 14604

Yesterday's Muse Books
32 West Main St.
Webster, NY 14580

Nashville Souvenirs
2613 McGavock Pk,
Nashville, TN 37214

Barnes & Noble
805 Eastview Mall,
Victor, NY 14564

Barnes & Noble
1 Walden Galleria g113,
Buffalo, NY 14225

Abundance Food Co-op
571 South Ave,
Rochester, NY 14620

Union Tavern
4565 Culver Rd,
Irondequoit, NY 14622

DATES IN THE STATES

A COUPLE TRAVELING THE UNITED
STATES ON A BUDGET

datesinthestates.com

✉

datesinthestatesblog@gmail.com

📍

Based in Rochester, NY

CONNECT WITH US ON SOCIAL!
@DATESINTHESTATES